This Book Belongs To:

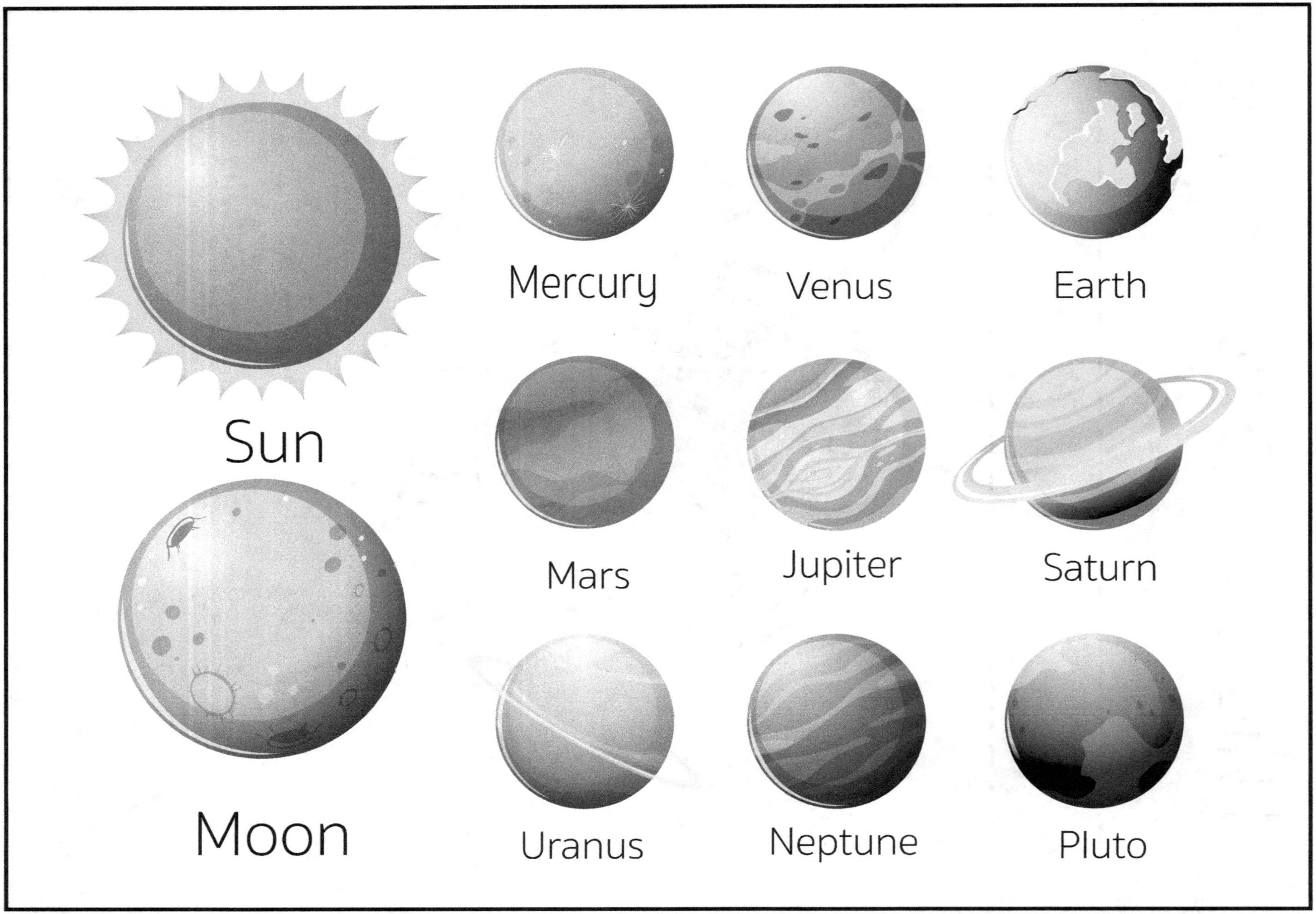
Sun
Mercury
Venus
Earth
Mars
Jupiter
Saturn
Moon
Uranus
Neptune
Pluto

SATURN

SUN

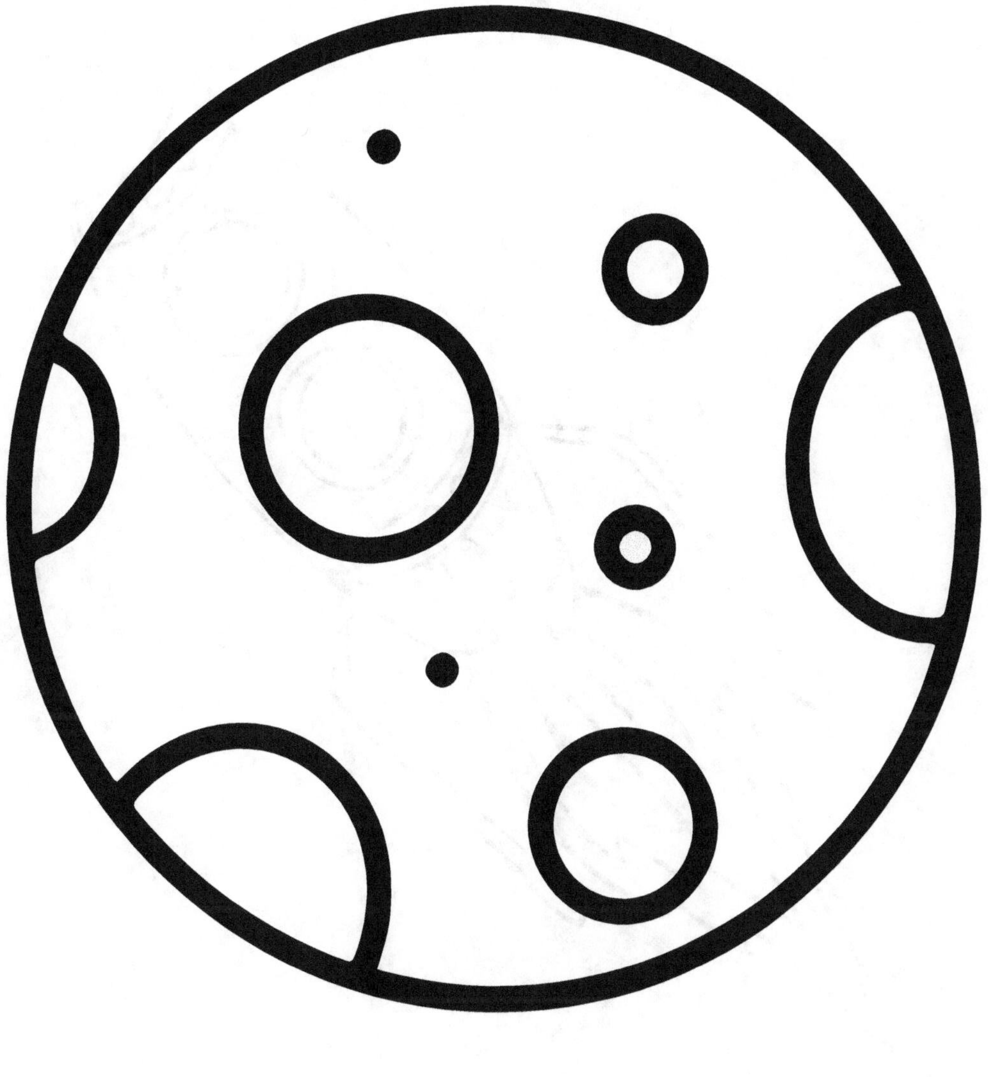

MOON

ROCKET

URANUS

VENUS

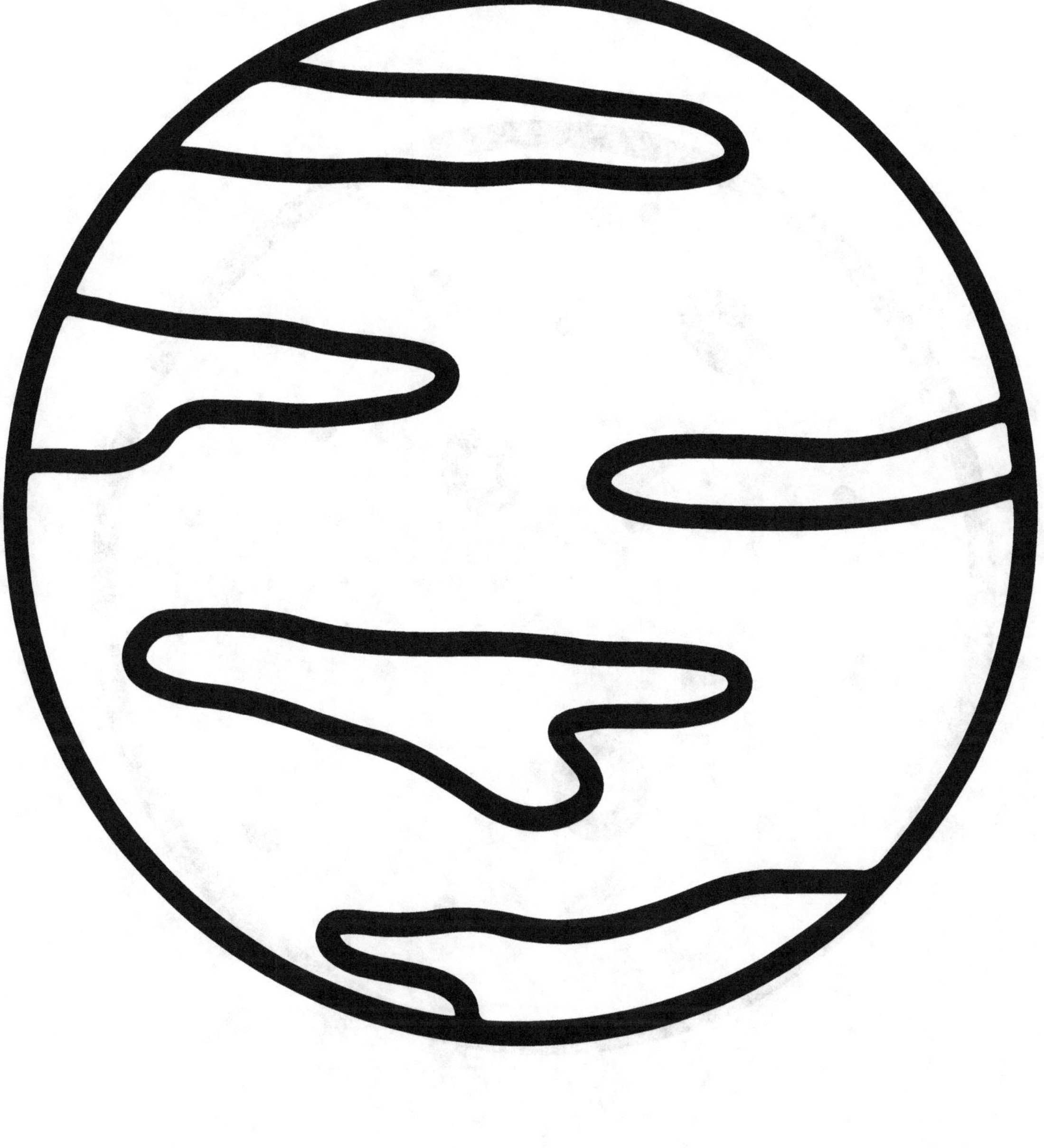

NEPTUNE

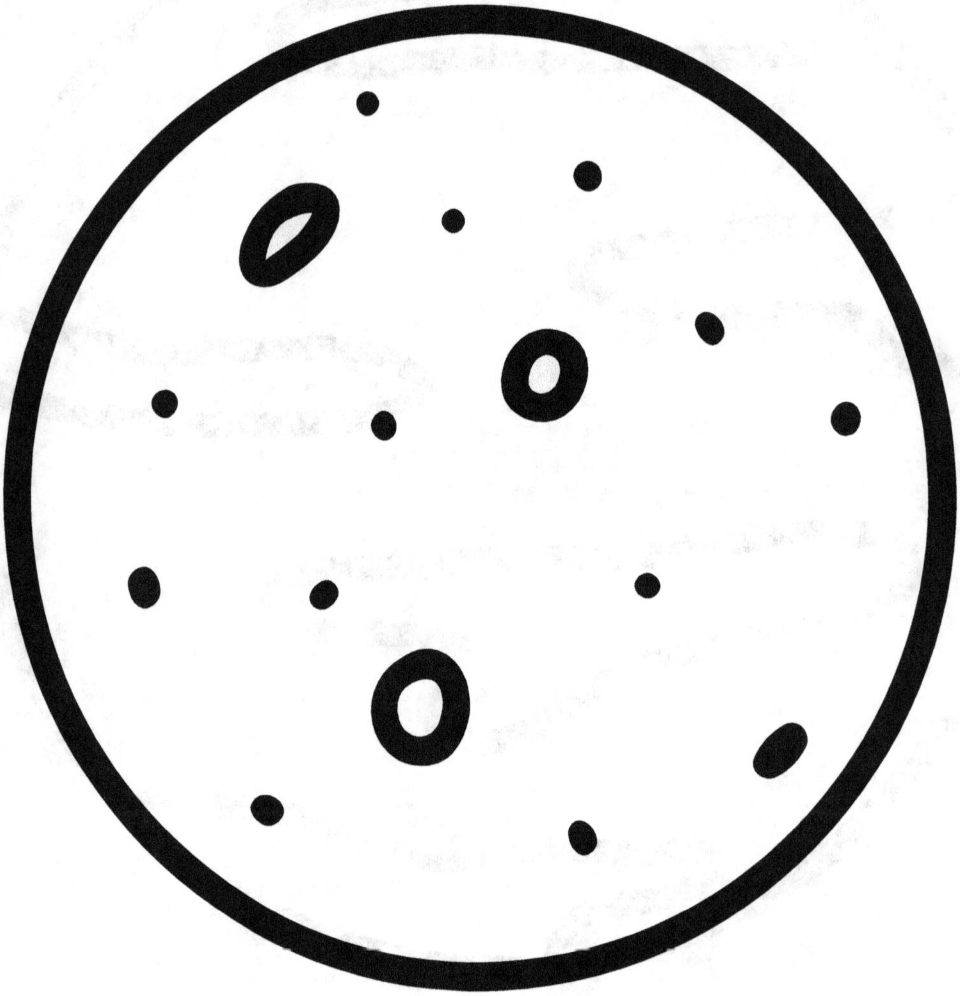

PLUTO

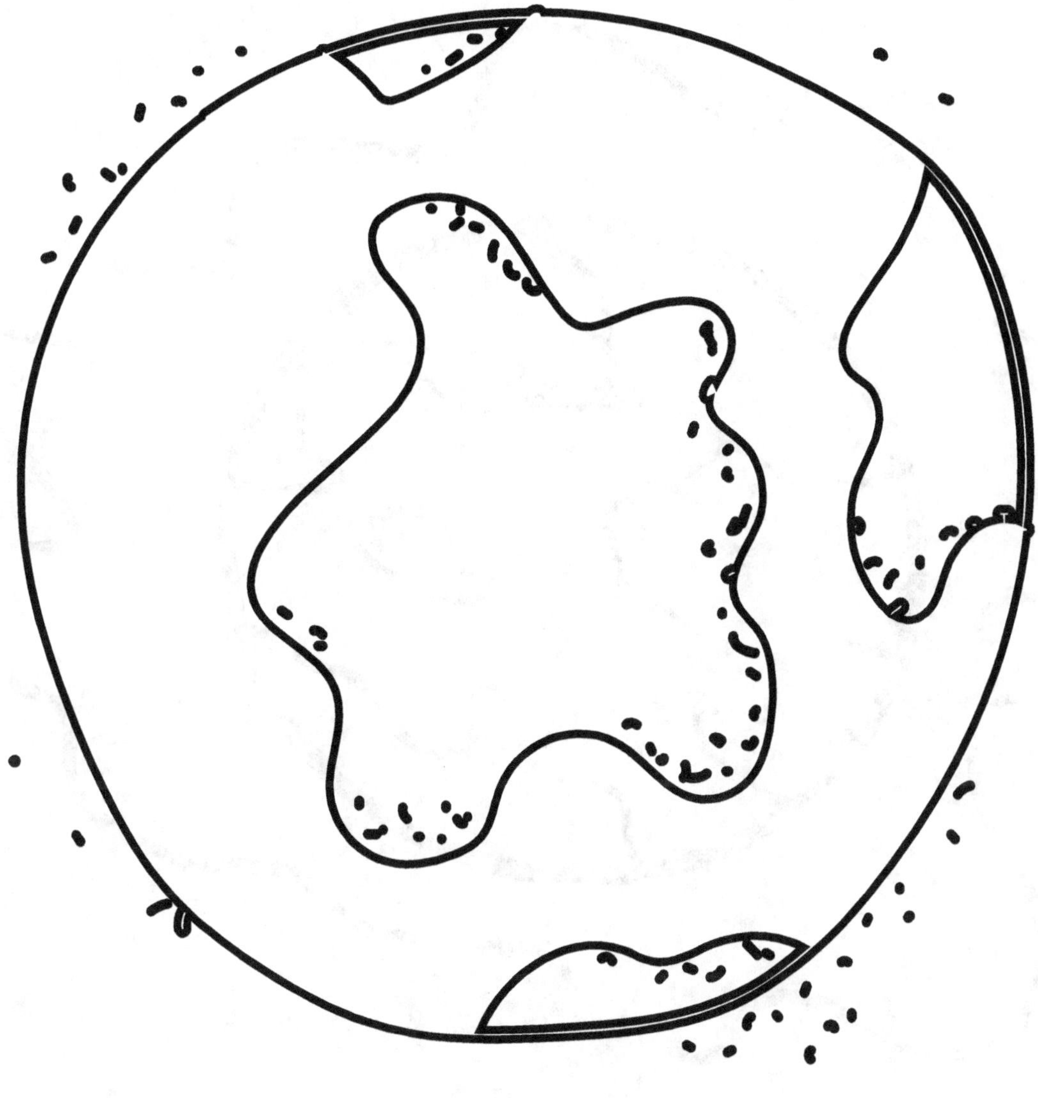

EARTH

MARS

MERCURY

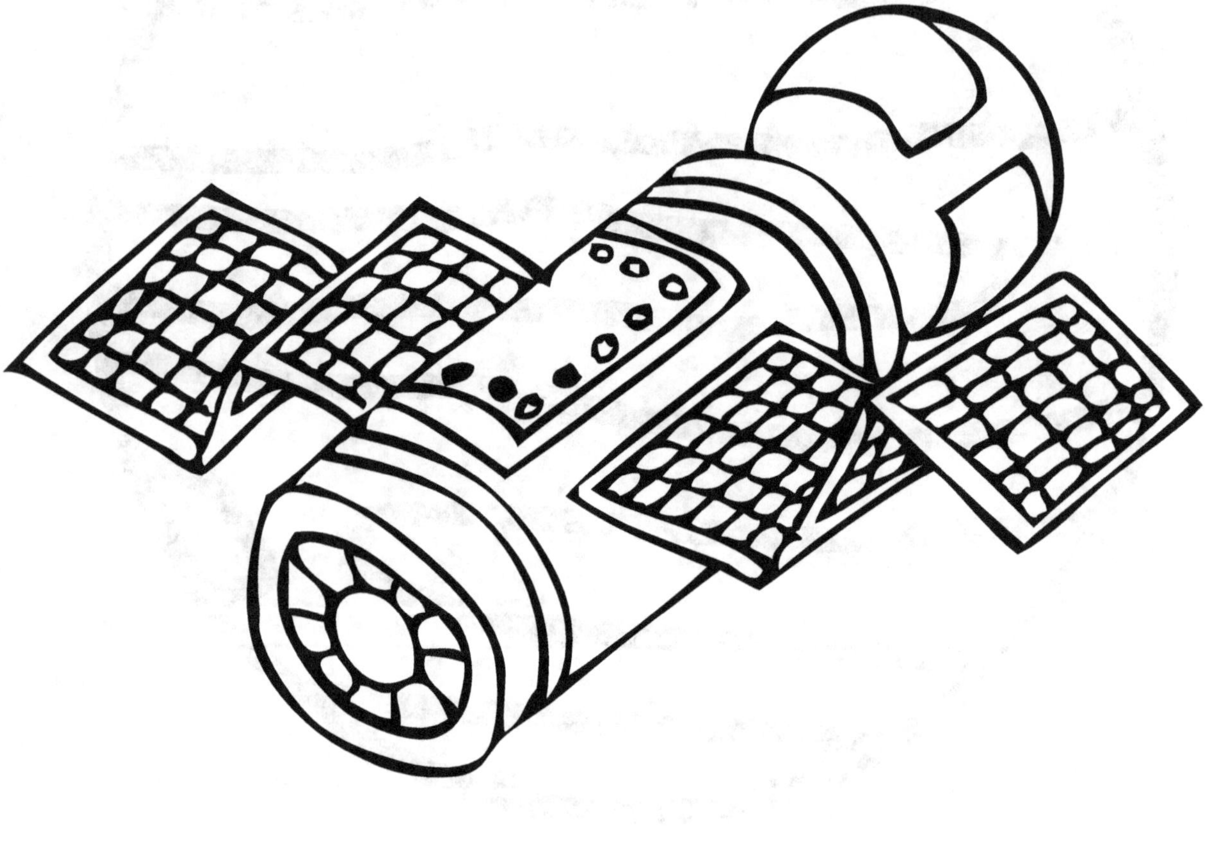

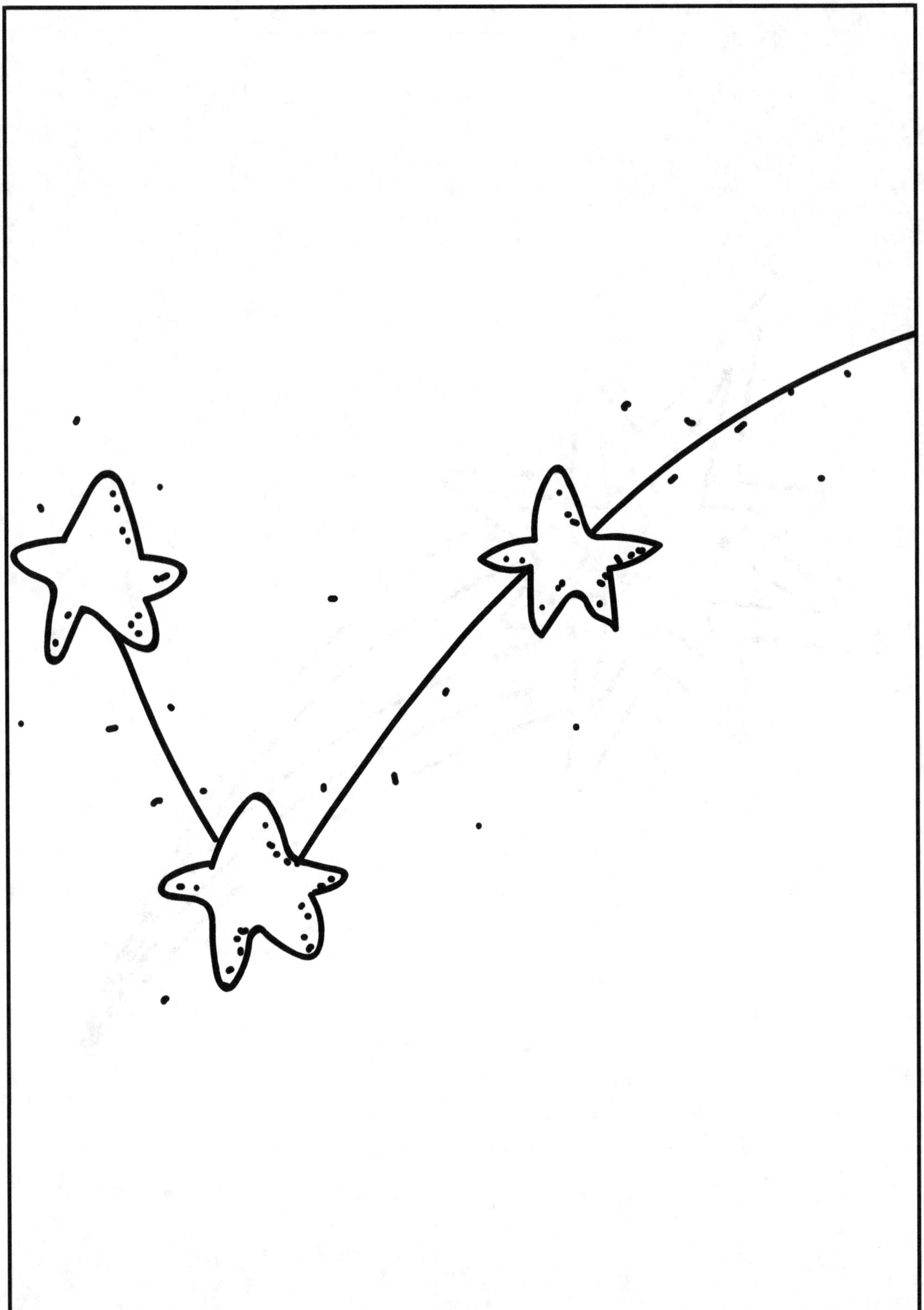

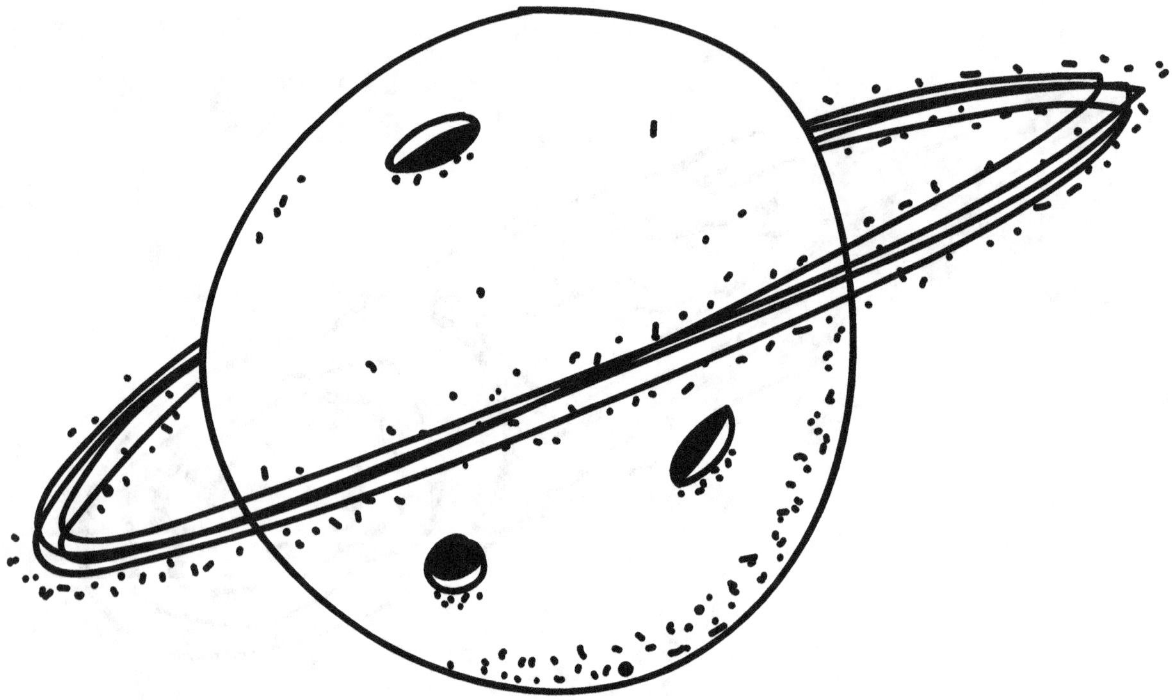

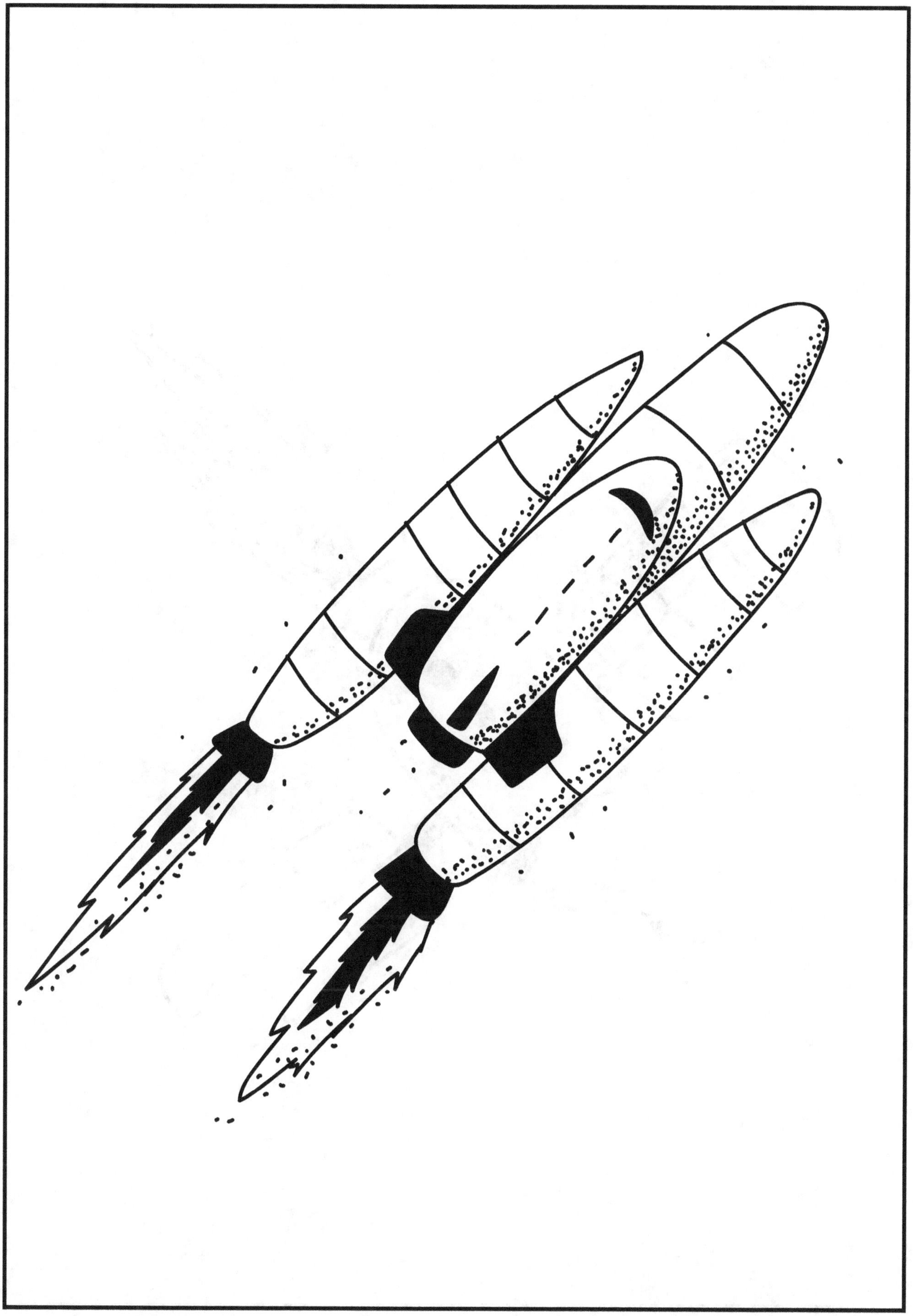

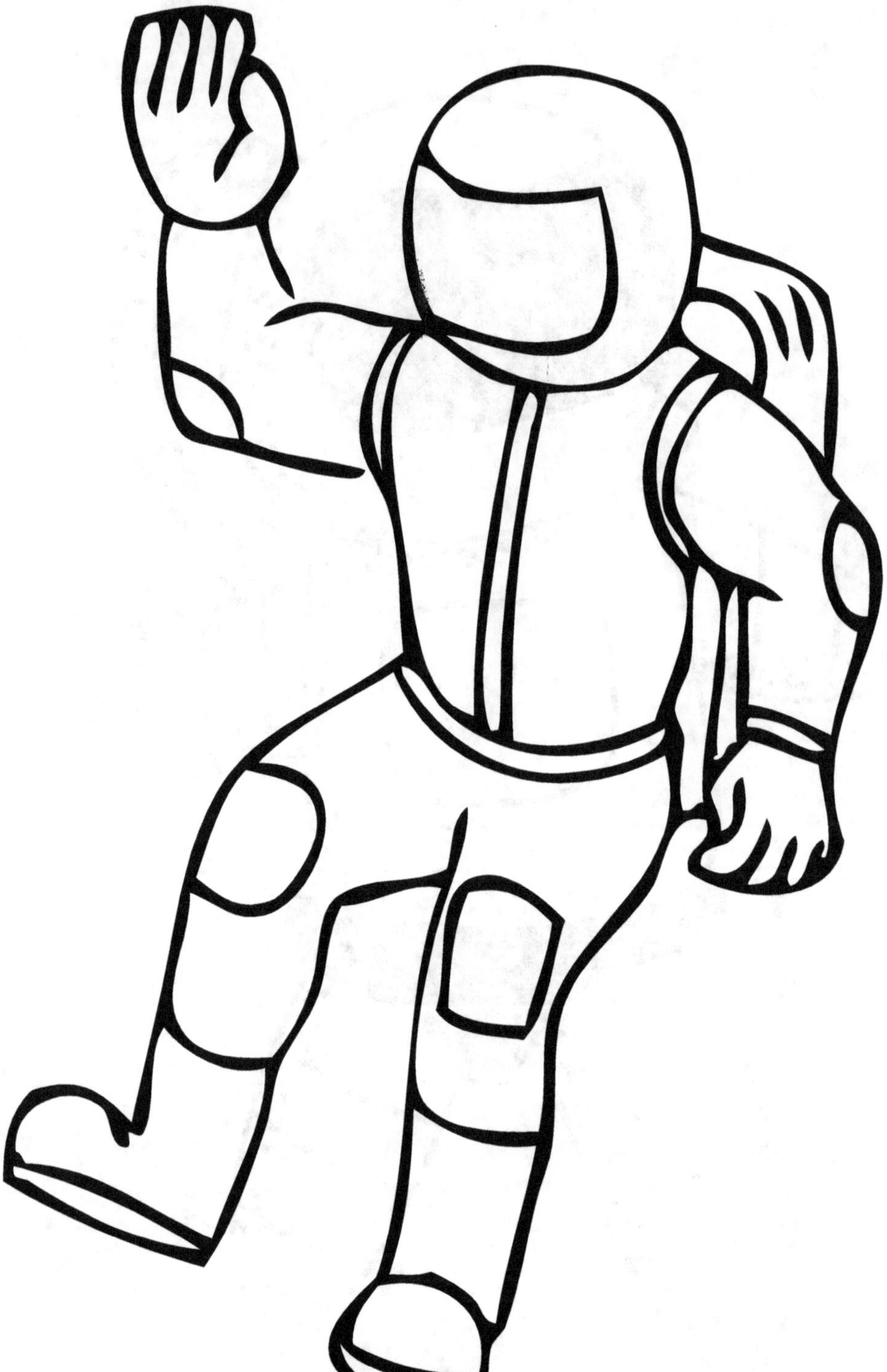

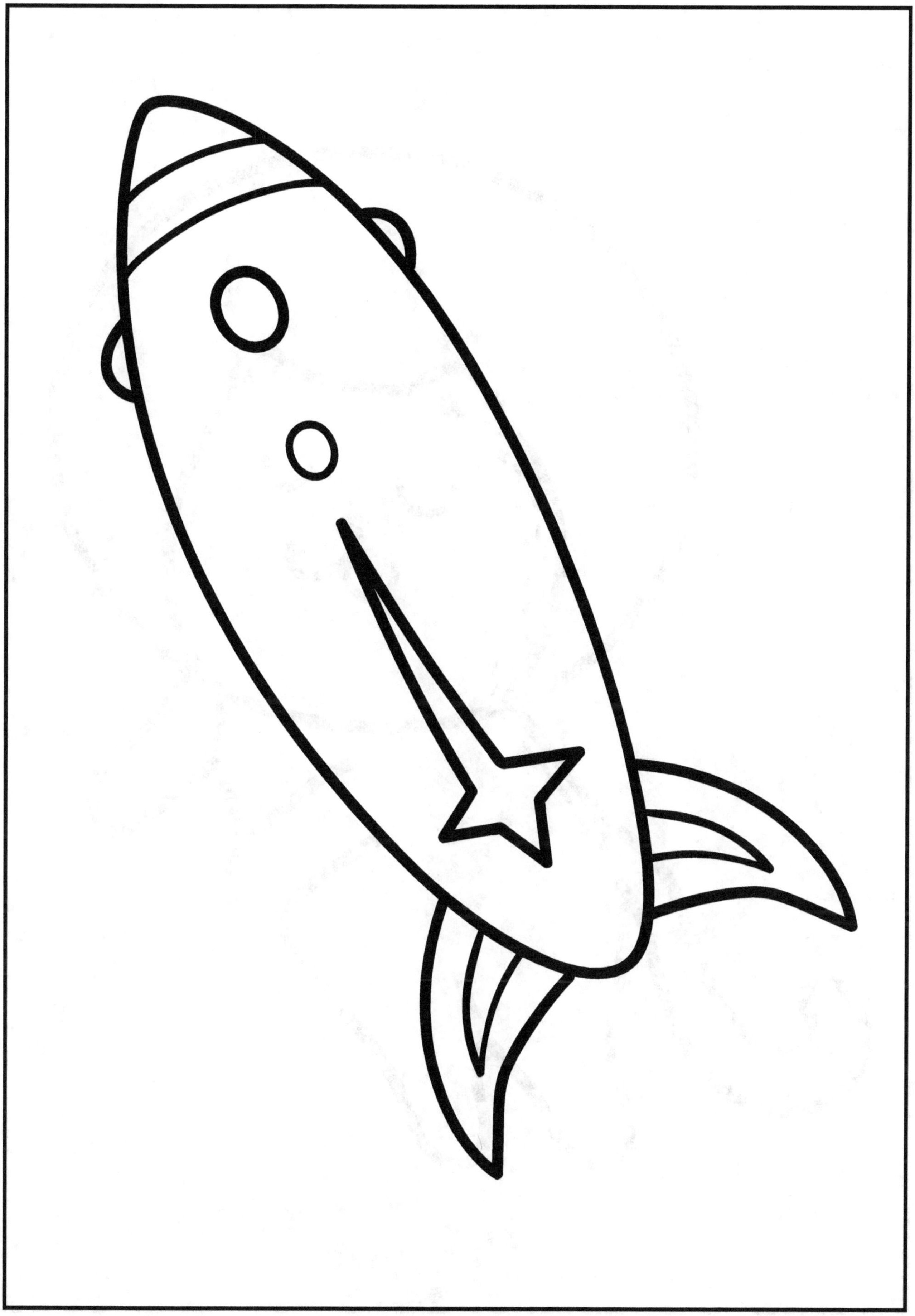

www.ingramcontent.com/pod-product-compliance
Lightning Source LLC
Chambersburg PA
CBHW080629220526
45467CB00011B/3440
* 9 7 9 8 7 0 9 1 9 6 0 8 7 *